The Second Portrait of a Seaside Town

The Second Portrait of a Seaside Town

Historic Photographs of WHITSTABLE

From the

Douglas West

Collection

First Printed   January 1987
Second Edition   August 1989

© DOUGLAS WEST

All rights reserved. No part of this book
may be produced in any way without
permission from the publishers.

Paperback ISBN 0 9508564 6 0
Hardback   ISBN 0 9508564 7 9

Text set in Baskerville 11pt

Printed and Published in Great Britain by
Emprint Publications, 9 Harbour Street, Whitstable, Kent CT5 1AG

The old order changeth, yielding place to new.

Tennyson. (Morte d'Arthur)

WHITSTABLE

I make no apology for this second and companion book of the photographic history of Whitstable. I had, perforce, to omit some photographs from the first book to make it a manageable size. They are here recorded together with dramatic pictures of the various floods and frozen seas. Also included are some of the official photographs of the bomb damage suffered by Whitstable in the Second World War. Recorded too are photographs of shops and their owners, photographs showing graphically the prices of the Sunday joint in the early days of this century and the exodus to the hop gardens of the hop-pickers who made the annual event a holiday — a holiday that is no longer possible. Recorded too are some of the Whitstable builders of long ago, all helping to make the character of Whitstable, a seafaring town of a seafaring nation.

Many artists have visited and made homes here. J. M. W. Turner came here to sketch the incomparable sunsets across the sea with Sheppey in the distance. Laurence Irving had a studio in the Borstal Hill Mill and entertained leading members of the theatrical profession there. Somerset Maugham too, who wrote of a thinly disguised 'Blackstable' and its people. Dan Sherrin, Charlie Chester, Peter Cushing and Trader Horn all found homes here and Charles Dickens visited Whitstable in the summer of 1859. We should be proud of our heritage.

The production of these two books has given me untold pleasure and I hope and trust they will give the people of Whitstable similar delight.

Douglas West

ACKNOWLEDGEMENTS

Mr. Wallace Harvey for his invaluable help in the production of this second book.

The "Whitstable Times and Tankerton Press".

The National Motor Museum at Beaulieu.

The British Broadcasting Corporation.

All the people of Whitstable who have contributed by loaning historic photographs and without whose help this book would not have been possible.

BIBLIOGRAPHY

"Whitstable Times"

Parish Church of St. Alphege, Whitstable. *Wallace Harvey*

Whitstable and the French Prisoners of War. *Wallace Harvey*

Kellys Directory

Blue Book Directory

A reproduction of an 1819 map shows in details the copperas works and also the location of three Whitstable windmills — Feakins Mill in Belmont Road, the Borstal Hill Mill and the Martindown Mill which was sited just off Martindown Road at the top of Borstal Hill. The salt pans are shown too — a double row of salt pans are seen more clearly in the map overleaf. It will be noticed that there is no direct road from Tankerton Castle to Swalecliffe, this was not constructed until the end of the century, until then one had to go via Church Street.

A larger scale map of approximately the same date showing in more detail the location of the Whitstable salt pans. The three main dykes which cross what is now the Seasalter Golf Club links. All this land was flooded at the spring tides and Oxford Street was virtually the shore line. The construction of the Island Wall and Sea Wall allowed the land to be drained and developed. The Middle Wall was constructed in 1583 but it only protected the High Street. Further protection was made when Island Wall was constructed in 1798—1806 by John Knott, Stephen Salisbury and Edward Foad. Likewise the Sea Wall which was constructed by the Commissioners of Sewers in 1780. You will notice from the map that the development is all on the landward side of the Middle Wall.

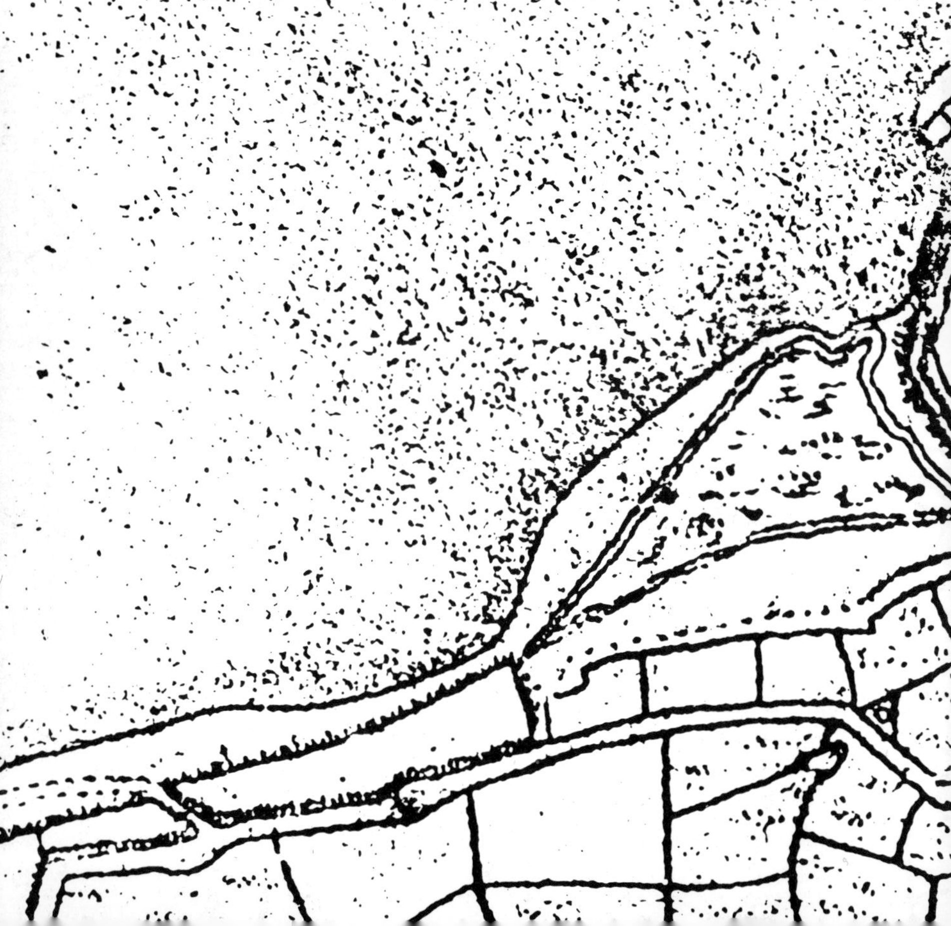

An aerial photograph of practically the whole of the Seasalter Golf Club course. Taken in 1935 it shows also the Boating Lake (run by Mr. Scammell) which today is filled in and built over. Collingwood Road and Cornwallis Circle have at this time yet to be built. This whole area was, several hundred years before given over to reclaiming salt from the sea by flooding the area and then evaporating part at a time to salt pans, which was an important industry at the time. Even in fairly recent times the sea flooded this part of Whitstable at Spring Tides right up to Oxford Street until the various sea walls — Island Wall and Sea Wall enabled the land to be developed and built over. This area is still called 'The Salts'. In severe storms these walls have since proved ineffective which has necessitated the construction of a modern and much higher wall. At this time the Boating Lake was enjoyed by countless youngsters. It is now all filled in and the Whitstable Squash Rackets Club has been built on the centre part and fronting the road. The Squash Rackets Club is now run by Mr. and Mrs. Hurdle. Mrs. Shirley Hurdle is the daughter of Frank Reeves, one of the large Reeves family. His uncle was George Reeves the builder who developed Chestfield in the 1920's. Another uncle, Stanley Reeves, also a builder, lived opposite the flagstaff on Marine Parade. Before the second world war he employed many men in the building trade. It was Stanley Reeves who rebuilt the front of the Congregational Church.

One of the dykes that crossed the golf course ran into this small lake which was developed by Mr. Dick Scammell who lived in 'Kingfisher' by the side of the lake, now of course filled in. It was a centre for the holiday-makers in this part of the town.

The West End of Whitstable

Seasalter Boating Lake

Harbour House here photographed about 1890 in close proximity to the coke ovens and the chimneys. All have now disappeared and the area is now covered by Bretts stone and asphalt processing plant and various warehouses. The coke ovens were built in 1847 and demolished in 1892 having stood for 45 years. The bricks (a million of them) were used as hardcore for the construction of Tankerton Road, one of the first roads to be constructed by the new Tankerton Estate which was formed in 1890.

This is the first known photograph of the Whitstable postmen — taken in 1904, the year that Mr. Geo Reeves built the fine post office in the High Street. It shows the postmaster Mr. William Nichols in the centre with his wife and staff. Mr. Nichols died three years later and his widow took over a sub-post office in St. Georges Street, Canterbury (where the ABC Cinema is now). The postmen of those days always wore a uniform — the hard hat was of a unique and unmistakable design. A postcard posted in the morning was delivered at teatime the same day — all for a halfpenny! There was only one postman in Whitstable in 1821.

Harbour House

Whitstable Postmen

A typical photograph of Whitstable harbour in the 1890's. Colliers are lined up, stem to stern, discharging coal from the north of England. It is a good photograph too of the old engine house and its chimney which has lost its black smoke-soiled top. A harbour light was fitted in 1846 which was visible for 10 miles. The engine was not then required as railway engines were now more powerful and could travel the whole distance between Whitstable and Canterbury. A Thames barge is seen with sails aloft and travelling light leaving the harbour mouth. The engine house is now completely demolished.

This capstan situated at the end of the East Quay has now disappeared as has also the flagstaff outside the Seasalter and Ham Oyster Fishery Co's premises in the harbour. This is a very early photograph taken in the latter part of the 19th century. Oyster fishermen are seen carrying empty butter tubs later to be filled with oysters for transport. Whitstable oysters had an enviable reputation as the finest in the world. (See photographs on page 65 in the author's first book "Portrait of a Seaside Town").

The Harbour

The East Quay Capstan

This High Street scene shows the earliest photograph of the "Ship Centurian Inn" on the extreme right. Bill Gammon, the licensee, an old sailor, is seen outside with his wife. The building was completely rebuilt in 1913. Originally called "The Ship" "Centurian" was added later. Shops have been built in the bottom of the following cottages, mostly roofs were not altered. Mr. Harold Wilman, who had a shop here, fitted large glass windows for his furniture displays. It was one of the first shops to be lit by electricity, a 110V private supply. The tall building at the end of this row of cottages is a butchers shop as it still is (Theobalds). The slaughter house still stands down Skinners Alley and dates back to the beginning of the 19th century. On the opposite side of the road are some of the original weather-boarded buildings that lined Whitstable Street. "Skinners Alley" was named after Mr. W. P. Skinner who had a gentlemans outfitters shop on the corner where Griffeys is now.

Nothing like a fire to attract a crowd — an exciting event not to be missed in those days. This one was in the building, which is now the Trustee Savings Bank, in the early 1900's. This too was in the days of the manual fire engine drawn by two horses. The policeman seems not to be worried by the crowd blocking the High Street — the slow-moving traffic in those days could always go round the back streets. There was always plenty of help to man the pump whenever the water supply was from a pond etc. In those days too it will be noticed that you weren't properly dressed if you weren't wearing a hat!

High Street

Fire in the High Street

The popular "Down Your Way" programme of the BBC visited Whitstable in August 1949 and Richard Dimbleby who presented the programme is seen here sampling Whitstable oysters at the Whitstable Oyster Fishery Company's premises on the Horsebridge. The programme was transmitted at the beginning of the oyster season on the 4th September 1949. He was also taken to the Castle and climbed to the top of the tower where there is a good view over the town. Whitstable was visited by the "Down Your Way" team again in 1981 and the programme was transmitted on Radio 4 on the 18th of October of that year.

Torrential rain fell on the town this day in August 1939, flooding this part of the High Street and all but entering the shops. The row of shops is very interesting because the Maypole Dairy Co. has taken the place of Surmans the butchers, to be followed in turn by the Trustee Savings Bank and later still by Johnnies the greengrocers. Next door is Mr. Butcher the baker now (1986) Wetherleys. The boarded up shop was Holdens the jewellers, now moved to the opposite side of the road and lastly Barclays Bank which has since been demolished and rebuilt on the same site but to a deeper building line. War was now imminent and after hostilities a major reconstruction of the sewers was undertaken in the town.

'Down Your Way'

Flooding in the High Street

Black Cottages, Swalecliffe

Swalecliffe

These timbered and tarred cottages date from the 16th century and were situated along St. Johns Road, Swalecliffe. In the early 17th century Mr. Edmond Rouse lived here — his daughter Alexandra was born at the Black Cottage on 10 September 1636. Mr. Rouse with Thomas Gold established copperas works in Whitstable about 1625. There were four copperas works in Whitstable at this time. The Tea Gardens on Tower Hill was one site, others were where the Wynn Ellis almshouses now stand, the Tankerton Tower and the outlets at the Harbour and Beach Walk. Copperas (copper sulphate) was used extensively in the dyeing and ink making industries. The Black Cottages were demolished in 1937/8 and unfortunately the valuable timbers were destroyed in the process. Modern houses now occupy the site.

This early photograph of the junction of Herne Bay Road and Chestfield Road was taken c1900. The cottage on the right was later used as a surgery for Doctors Callender and Glynn but is now demolished. The Broadway was later constructed and the roadway widened. The Swalecliffe and Chestfield railway station was not built until 1930 when Mr. Geo Reeves, a Whitstable builder, developed Chestfield village and Chestfield Golf Club which was opened on 5th May 1924.

Annual Public House Outings

During the summer months a public house outing was a very popular and well attended event which a number of pubs organised. Before the advent of the motor coach the usual vehicle was a two or four horse brake which can be seen in the "Guinea Inn" outing which was photographed around 1914. These were quite high vehicles and were used extensively for childrens school treats which were often held in a local farmers field. For the "Royal Sovereign" public house outing in Victoria Street, the new Native Motor Coach was used, the driver being Mr. Rigden who was the fire engine driver for many years. This photograph was taken in the 1920's. Most of these men were in the building trade. In these days too the larger builders in the town had similar annual outings. Often the annual holidays were taken in the winter so the summer outing was a real treat.

The First Whitstable Girl Guides was formed in 1918 by Miss Sylvia Watkins, whose brother Claude was vicar of St. Alphege from 1916 to 1921. This photograph was taken in 1927 when his brother Wilfrid was in turn vicar from 1921 to 1927. Miss Watkins is sitting behind the mascot in the centre of the group which was taken outside the Endowed School. She handed over to her sister Joyce who is seen sitting next to her on the left. The guide holding the shield is Elsie Whorlow and her sister Lilian is the Lieutenant sitting immediately behind her. The guide holding the cup is Doris Keam and the guide holding the flag on the extreme right is Beatrice Bicker. There must be many who can be identified in this group, some still living in Whitstable.

An early photograph of the Fife Drum and Bugle Band which later developed into the Whitstable Naval Cadet Band — the oldest Sea Cadet unit in the country, which was formed in 1854. The diversity of the age of the members is noticeable. Of interest too is the uniform of the two police constables PC399 on the left and PC310 on the right. The police of those days seem not to miss a chance to 'get into the picture'.

Girl Guides

Fife & Drum Band

This Congregational Church outing photographed c1911 is a wonderful study of the ladies' hats of the period. Mr. George E. Foad who built the Church at Swalecliffe, the Salvation Army Hall and the Catholic Church is seen sitting fourth from the right in the second row. Mr. Church was another well-known Whitstable tradesman who had a furniture and general hardware shop where the Fine Fare supermarket is now. He is seen in a dark suit at the left-hand of the fourth row. The group was arranged on and around a farm cart which was almost certainly used to transport some members to the venue.

Fifty young hopefuls, in a competition at the Castle Pleasure Gardens, are in their best party dresses. There was dancing too for the grown-ups in the evening with fairy lights hung around. One cannot help comparing these laughing children with their counterparts 50—60 years earlier when there was much poverty in the town. This area is now all taken over with laid-out gardens. But what were three little boys doing amongst all that feminine charm? The gardens were opened to the public in 1935. All this has now gone though the gardens are public property and are very attractive and a real asset to the town.

Congregational Church Outing c1911

The Castle Pleasure Gardens

Priest & Sow Corner

West End Regatta

In the 1920's when this photograph was taken the Priest and Sow corner boasted a small tea garden and a miniature golf course. Houses started to appear along Herne Bay Road thus connecting the ancient village of Swalecliffe to the town of Whitstable. No definite information exists with regard to this peculiar name given to the area. It could be a corruption of an ancient name. Certainly a public house of this name never existed here. Mr. Harvey informs us it could be a corruption of three languages, the Saxon 'Preost' — a priest or dedicated man, the Anglo Saxon or Old English 'tan' from 'tanjan' — a fire and the Danish 'how' — a boundary. So there may well have been a beacon here in the past. We shall probably never know for certain.

Here is a cross-section of Whitstable people watching the West End Regatta off the West Beach. The Whitstable Regatta was always held off the Tankerton Slopes which made a good grandstand. The West End Regatta was a smaller affair and was largely supported by the Sea Cadets and Sea Scouts. This photograph shows the everyday costume of the early 1900's. Large crowds gathered at every form of entertainment in those days. In the summer a small band used to play in a corrugated iron-roofed shelter near Wave Crest. Regattas have been held in Whitstable for almost 200 years. The first one was held on 7 August 1792.

1897 FLOOD

The first Whitstable flood to be photographed happened on 29th November 1897. The results must have been very similar to the 1953 flood, although there were not so many people and houses at that time. The photographs show the height of the flood along the length of Nelson Road which reached the middle sash of the lower windows. It must be remembered that a hundred years earlier this whole area was subject to flooding right up to the houses in Oxford Street during Spring tides, indeed Oxford Street was literally the shore line. The construction of Middle Wall, Island Wall and Sea Wall was to prevent such flooding. Even with the construction of a concrete wall the whole event was to be repeated 56 years later. But there was a warning on 1st March 1949 when huge waves topped the wall and which broke over the top of the old Neptune public house on the Marine Terrace flooding Waterloo Road. About a dozen photographs exist of the 1897 flood, some of which are recorded here.

The flooded "Salts" with few houses on the lower Island Wall. A couple of shipyards were here at this time, all have gone now. This whole area is now the Seasalter Golf Club which was formed twelve years later in 1909.

The height of the flood water is plainly visible on the extreme right in this valuable photograph of 1897 showing Nelson Road from the Island Wall. Bowler hats seemed to be popular in those days — even the young fireman is wearing one.

This photograph was taken from the Oxford Street end of Nelson Road. It shows that the flood covered walls and railings in front of the houses and even reached the centre sashes of the windows.

A view of the "Salts" from Island Wall. The house surrounded with water is in Nelson Road. This end of the road was the last to be built on. The long wall on the extreme left is at the rear of the coastguard houses.

This interesting photograph of Reeves Beach shows damage to the foundations of the houses on Sea Wall. The architecture too is remarkable.

Again in this photograph the flood water has darkened the houses in Island Wall to the height of the middle sashes. The crowd is apparently watching a rescue with a precariously placed ladder to an upstairs window.

Another view of the "Salts". The half-constructed Wave Crest is in the distance. The houses on the right are the rear of Nelson Road. Collingwood Road has yet to be built.

1949 FLOOD

During this flood I set out to photograph the waves breaking over the sea wall at some real risk when photographing along the beach. A number of these photographs have never been published. This flood has been largely forgotten because of the major flood which happened four years later, but it was an ominous warning.

The sea here is seen breaking over the Horsebridge. The wall has since been raised and flood gates fitted.

The power of the storm-lashed waves is shown in this photograph along the beach of Sea Wall. The noise of the undertow as the waves swept back taking tons of beach with them was really frightening.

Waves are seen breaking over the sea wall at the height of the storm. This part of the Whitstable shore took a terrific battering.

The height of the waves is vividly pictured here breaking over the top of the "Old Neptune" public house and swirling over the sea wall along Marine Terrace.

All these cottages have now disappeared. In their place is the Over 60's Rest Centre and the newly built Saltings homes.

Water pours over Island Wall, flooding the houses opposite and also Waterloo Road.

The sea cascades over the sea wall at Marine Terrace. The "Old Neptune" public house stands in the centre of the storm-lashed waves.

1953 FLOOD

"The olde sea wall (he cried) is downe,
The rising tide comes on apace,
And boats adrift in yonder towne
Go sailing uppe the market-place."

Jean Ingelow
(The high tide on the coast of Lincolnshire, 1571)

On that fateful Sunday morning of 1 February 1953 I arrived at my Studio to find the shop and workrooms in 2 feet of water. A very heavy oak settle was floating on its back along with other flotsam. There was a quiet calm over the town, there was no traffic or buses and only one or two people standing in the High Street doorways.

There was little I could do and fortunately all my cameras and film stock were above flood level so, standing in water to the top of my wellingtons I set forth to photograph this tragic happening. The whole day was spent photographing every area and aspect of the flood. It was the most dramatic days work I had ever done. The fortitude of the Whitstable people in the face of this nightmare was tremendous — there was no panic — just friendly helpers rescuing people from windows who were trapped in upstairs rooms.

Out at Seasalter the sea wall was breached, cattle drowned and the main railway line destroyed. This necessitated the reopening of the Whitstable to Canterbury railway which had been officially closed the previous November.

Praise must deservedly go to the Fire Brigade who had the seemingly impossible task of pumping all that water back into the sea. Every available pump for miles around was brought into use and dozens of hoses were draped over the sea walls to reduce the level of flood water in the town.

To aid and alleviate the suffering of the flooded victims a special fund was opened by the Lord Mayor of London Sir Rupert de la Bere. He visited the town on 20 April 1953 and was entertained to lunch by the Whitstable Urban District Council at the Tankerton Hotel.

The following photographs testify to the enormity of this disaster and of the ordeal suffered by so many in the early hours of that dramatic Sunday morning. Let us hope that this terrible happening will never be repeated.

Mr. Keith Foster who, with fisherman Victor Davis rescued a hundred people that morning. They carried a rowing boat from the harbour to the end of Middle Wall where a couple, Mr. & Mrs. Hobden, who had only been married the day before, were trapped in their upstairs room at Rye's furniture store, now occupied by Ansleys the builders. They lost a lot of wedding presents that night. The photograph included here shows Mr. Foster on the left holding the ladder and Vic Davis on the right rescuing the occupants of a cottage No. 86 Middle Wall, a mother and her baby together with a child still clutching her teddy bear. Later the cat was also lowered into the boat by a helpful army sergeant. The baby got a bit wet when the ladder pushed the boat away from the house, but all was well in the end. This cottage has now disappeared and the Middle Wall car park takes its place. To clear the area the fire brigade set fire to some of the cottages for fire practice.

A really historic photograph. All these cottages have disappeared and the area is now the Middle Wall car park. A woman is being lowered on to the shoulders of a rescuer who in turn is standing in an unsteady rowing boat. The "Wall Tavern" can be seen on the extreme right. Rescues like this were going on all over this part of the town.

Nelson Road from Island Wall. Helpers and rescuers in rowing boats did wonderful work reassuring the nervous and apprehensive. Two thousand people were made homeless and a reception and rest centre was set up in the Boys School in Oxford Street. Mrs. Sinclair of Nelson Road, with her mother and family, spent 10 hours in an upstairs bedroom before being rescued by boat. Flood water had reached half-way up the stairs.

Middle Wall

Nelson Road

The Salts

High Street

The "Salts" with the Seasalter Golf Clubhouse where the floodwater reached the gutters and cars were completely submerged. Dramatic rescues were made in Collingwood Road which was being built at this time. Wallace Harvey and Jack Philpot made several attempts to reach people here. Gilbert Gremo lowered his wife and two children from a bedroom window and Mr. & Mrs. Gilbert Cawley and their son were likewise rescued.

The High Street deserted and silent on that Sunday morning looking more like a river than a highway. Water here reached about three feet deep. There were few residents in the High Street, it being all shops and offices. The Westminster Bank is on the extreme right of the photograph.

West Beach

The Old Neptune

West Beach as always suffered severe damage. The front of this building has been demolished. Dozens of beach huts were damaged here and blown and floated on to the Seasalter Golf Course. Great holes were torn in the wall that crosses the golf course.

The lower part of the "Old Neptune" public house being torn apart by the storm. This unique old pub sited actually on the beach has suffered much damage over the years. Only a few sturdy posts are keeping the building from crashing into the sea.

A dramatic rescue in Middle Wall. A headscarfed lady descends a ladder into a rowing boat. Another is already down clutching a holdall with a few essentials. These two weatherboard cottages are the only ones left in this part of Middle Wall.

Rescue work goes on in the Oxford Street end of Nelson Road, while a little girl waits patiently by the only means of transport along this river on that fateful Sunday morning.

Mr. Douglas West photographed by his colleague Mr. Eric Hall in the High Street, early on that Sunday morning. Other members of the staff turned up to help but there was nothing that could be done until the flood water had gone.

The Island Wall junction with Waterloo Road. The scene is now a peaceful sunlit Sunday morning after a night of terror with every rowing boat in great demand.

An elderly gentleman waits his turn to be helped to safety, but the dog comes first in this Nelson Road rescue. It was rumoured that 17 cats went sailing by on a plank of wood in Nelson Road. The story was true, Mrs. Sinclair, who herself was rescued by boat, actually saw this incongruous scene. The cats were afterwards cared for by the R.S.P.C.A.

Island Wall

Nelson Road

Harbour House which was probably associated with the coke ovens with their huge chimneys which were located hard by. The old Harbour railway station inside the eastern harbour gates can be seen on the extreme right. The floodwater here reached almost to the top of the front door.

The sea wall at Seasalter collapsed under the extreme pressure of the sea, the marshes were flooded and many cattle were drowned. The main railway line to Faversham was destroyed and the importance of the old Whitstable to Canterbury line was realised so it was reopened for a month to enable repairs to be made to the main line.

Harbour House

Seasalter

Distressing scenes like this were seen all along the railway embankment at Seasalter. Mrs. McKeever, a farmer at Waterham, lost 130 ewes and Mr. Dadd of Pilgrims Lane could save only two from a herd of 30 T. T. cattle.

The dark line through the centre of the lower rooms in these Waterloo Road cottages shows, on the left of this photograph, the depth the flood water reached. All the cottages on the left have now gone and the Over 60's Rest Centre now occupies this site. In the distance half a dozen pumps are pumping the water back along Middle Wall to the sea.

Seasalter

Waterloo Road

The flooded interior of the Argosy Cinema in the High Street. (The old "Picture House" and now the Fine Fare supermarket).

The marines unloading equipment from landing craft at Seasalter for repairing the collapsed sea wall, aided by willing helpers.

The Argosy Cinema

Seasalter

The Lord Mayor of London, Sir Rupert de la Bere, accompanied by the Chairman of the Whitstable Urban District Council Cllr. J. P. Prangnell, who himself had to be rescued from his flooded home at Seasalter.

Handing out clothing etc. to flood victims in the Salvation Army Hall in the High Street. As always the Salvation Army is always ready and willing in times like this to really do something to alleviate suffering. A reception centre was set up in the Boys School in Oxford Street. The Minister of Health at the time, Dr. Charles Hill (the Radio Doctor) and Miss Pat Hornsby Smith, Parliamentary Secretary and Lord Harris visited the area and were satisfied with all arrangements.

Visit of the Lord Mayor of London

The Salvation Army Hall

The Church of St. John the Baptist, Swalecliffe — 1929

St. John's Convalescent Home, Marine Parade c1920

Swalecliffe Church was restored in 1875 by Mr. George E. Foad a Whitstable builder and undertaker. When the restoration was complete he nailed an 1872 halfpenny to the belfry. Fifty-four years later during a gale in January 1929 the belfry blew down and the halfpenny was recovered and handed back to Mr. Foad. It is now in the possession of the Rev. Leo Laker a maternal great grandson of Mr. Foad. There was a much older church here, the registers date back to 1558. The register for marriages and burials date from 1607. The foundation stone of the present building was laid on 8 July 1875 by the Earl of Aberdeen and consecrated by the Archbishop of Canterbury on 8 February 1876. The cost was £1,300. Designed by Robert Wheeler of Tunbridge Wells.

This building is the original Pier Pavilion which was immediately opposite the Pier which was demolished in 1912. When this photograph was taken the building was used, during the first world war and afterwards, as a convalescent home of the St. John Ambulance Brigade. Today it is part of the Royal Hotel (the Queens Bar).

(Even in those days pavements seem to be a source of trouble illustrated here by cracks and partial repairs!).

This photograph is interesting as it shows the very beginning of the Lawn Pavilion. The open-air stage can be seen at the end of the path complete with a concert party doing their best to entertain the elegant ladies of the period with their distinctive "Merry Widow" hats. This small stage was swept away a few years later and a marquee erected on the site. This too gave way to a permanent building in the 1920's which staged the "Jollity Boys", "Sandy Sandford Concert Party" etc. All this too has gone and the site is now designed as a picnic area. The Tankerton Hotel is on the extreme left and the Whitstable oyster fleet rides peacefully at anchor on the extreme right. Mr. Percival Barns took the photograph in the early 1900's.

Bathing Machines have been in use at Whitstable since 1768 — this is a good illustration of them, both single and double, on Tankerton Beach at the turn of the 19th century. They were towed by horses and winches were used to haul them up the beach, two of which can be seen in the foreground. During the summer there were probably a couple of dozen of these machines along the beaches. Also in the picture can be seen the sailing boats that local fishermen would take trippers out in for a sail along the coast. The small rowing boat on the right is seen to sport three umbrellas. Ladies of the time were careful of their complexions, even to the extent of using umbrellas on a trip in a rowing boat.

Tankerton Slopes

Tankerton Beach

The photographer had to climb the narrow winding stairway to the top of St. Alphege Church to get this photograph. It vividly shows that the High Street at this time (about 1880) was composed mainly of private houses, cottages for the most part, and some with bay windows had a wooden fence in front. The Salvation Army Hall had not yet been built nor the main Post Office (built 1904). In the top left of the picture the Baptist Church can be seen at the end of a long row of cottages in Middle Wall. The roofs in the immediate foreground are the "Queens Head" Inn, now Pirie & Cavender, booksellers.

This interesting photograph shows a domestic weatherboard building at the junction of Middle Wall and the High Street. Chester House now stands on this spot. The large brick building built in 1889 is now Days Garage (6 Oxford Street). It is uncertain what the notice on the donkey is for. It reads *"Help your worn and weary brother pulling hard against the strain. No outdoor relief. Wanted. Pauper and wife. Teetotlers only need apply. What a nuisance."* The schoolboy with the shopping basket, dressed in Norfolk jacket and Eton collar is typical of the well dressed schoolboy of the period (before World War I).

High Street

Oxford Street

This view of Tankerton Road looking towards Whitstable shows that the road is unmade with grass verges on each side (the road was made up around 1920). The shop on the extreme left is now the Tankerton Road Post Office. A row of shops have now replaced the two bungalows and the electric overhead cables show that the photograph was taken after 1914 when the Whitstable Electric Co. came into being. This area became the nucleus of the Tankerton shopping area in preference to the planned development in Pier Avenue some 20 years earlier.

Tankerton Circus a few years later. Shops have been built all along the road now and the Circus has been developed into an island roundabout. In recent years the centre has been enlarged, built higher and landscaped; the electric cables have now all gone underground.

Tankerton Road

Tankerton Circus

This Tankerton Beach photograph was probably taken on a Regatta Day or Bank Holiday about 1912. The building on the right is now the "Harbour Lights" bar and the building with the elaborate wooden balconies has all gone, the site was developed into the Continental Hotel. This area was always very popular as it is only a few minutes walk away from the Canterbury Railway and all around here were restaurants, tea booths and bazaars in Beach Road. The costumes suggest that the period was just before World War I.

This is an early photograph of the "Royal Naval Reserve" public house and the buildings to Terrys Lane. The public house at this time was only one house No. 28 but now occupies two, 28/30. This photograph was probably taken around 1890 after the name was changed from the "Rose" in 1876 in honour of the Royal Naval Reserve. This part of the High Street has been completely transformed by modern shops and offices, notably the Gas showrooms (No. 22) occupied by Hayes in the photograph and Lloyds Bank (14/16). It will be noticed that the "Duke of Cumberland" has only two dormer windows, today there are three but apart from that it has changed little since this photograph was taken. It was rebuilt after the fire of 8 October 1866.

Tankerton Beach

High Street

This view of St. Alphege Church in the High Street shows the original railings and the early planted trees. The front and the castellated tower were encased in stone to give the church a much better appearance. A Canterbury architect designed the church and the plans were approved and contracts signed in 1844. For almost a hundred years the church had only one bell, given by Mrs. Wynn Ellis. In 1920 a set of 8 brass tubular bells was presented but they were not very successful so in 1969 a peal of 6 bells were installed, the largest weighing more than 3 cwt. and were dedicated by the Bishop of Dover. The church interior was decorated by large murals by Capt. H. J. McGee of Whitstable and they are shown on Page 97 of Vol. 1. The building on the right of the church is the butcher's slaughter house in Skinners Alley which still stands, though it cannot now be seen from the High Street.

This is an early photograph of the Wesleyan Chapel and school-room in Argyle Road, known at this time as the Wesleyan Methodist Church and now as St. John's Methodist Church. The low brick wall and iron railings have all gone now, as well as the shrubs. The original chapel was a small wooden building in Middle Wall, built in 1819. Later a brick-built chapel was built in 1857. This was still not large enough so a modern church was built in Argyle Road and opened by the Rev. F. J. Johnson D.D. on 22 October 1868. The school room was built six years later in 1874. The old wooden building in Middle Wall was re-erected in Old House Field (between Sea Street and Harbour Street) but was burnt down during the great fire of 10 November 1869.

St. Alphege Church

St. John's Methodist Church

The arrival of the motor car in Whitstable. Here are two very early photographs, the first one shows Mr. E. Rigden in his 'White' steam car taken about 1906. The 'White' car was made about 1901 and the registration is an early London number which was used between January 1904 and May 1905. Mr. Rigden was a Whitstable butcher who had his shop where the Trustee Savings Bank in the High Street is now. The photograph was almost certainly taken at the rear of these premises.

The librarian of the Beaulieu Motor Museum thinks that this second photograph of a very early motor car in lone splendour travelling down the High Street is a Benz. It appears not to have any registration plate displayed on the front. Also it is not known who the two passengers are. Just behind the car is the junction of Middle Wall and the shuttered shop on the right is now occupied by the Save the Children Fund. The photograph was taken around the turn of the century. It will be remembered that Miss Dot Carson drove Queen Mary in a Vauxhall Car in 1915 and the design and performance was far advanced from the two cars here reproduced and in only a few years.

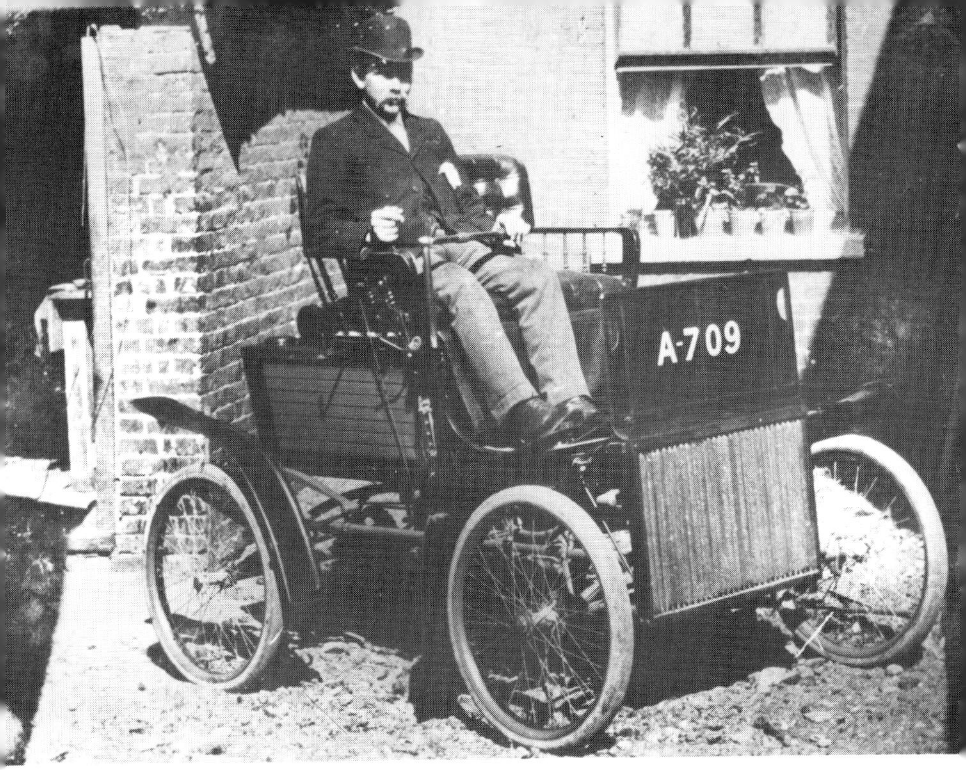

'Whites' Steam Car

High Street c1900

Surmans in the High Street

This photograph taken in the early 1920's shows the Christmas display put on by Mrs. Surman and Mr. Norris complete with striped butchers apron. Displays like this were usual in those days but of course are not now allowed. Pork was chopped in halves, lengthwise in the doorway hung by two hooks on the door posts, faggots with pease pudding were sold hot in your own basin, and meat was around 2/- per lb. This very early photograph shows the original Surmans shop No. 61 next door to the London and County Bank. When Surmans rebuilt their premises in 1928 they moved along one shop and No. 61 became the Maypole Dairy Co. Later this became the Trustee Savings Bank and is now a greengrocers.

Mr. Daly's grocers shop complete with four sides of bacon outside and father and son, complete with white aprons down to their shoes. Tea prices were 1s.6d. per lb. at this time. The shop, No. 87 High Street, was, years before, the original Whitstable Post Office. Mr. George Reeves built the modern post office opposite Gladstone Road in the High Street in 1904. It has now been moved to Gladstone Road. Mr. Daly's grocers shop was still in existence at the beginning of the second world war.

This photograph of Herbert Nicholls of the Whitstable Salvation Army was taken in 1904 when he was about 14 years old. In 1913 he was a builder in Harwich Street but in that year he emigrated to Toronto where he started a construction company with Mr. Milne. Another native of Whitstable Winifred Solly also emigrated to Toronto in May 1914 (her family were the Sollys who ran a china and glass shop at No.7 High Street, now Gaywoods Radio). The following year they were married and today Nicholls and Milne are one of the largest construction firms in Canada. Their son Roland Nicholls is President of the company. This is just one more instance, among many, of a Whitstable family making good overseas.

Daly's grocers shop in the High Street

Salvation Army Bandsman of 1904

FROZEN SEAS

"But the black north-easter,
Through the snowstorm hurled,
Drives our English hearts of oak
Seaward round the world."

Charles Kingsley.
(Ode to the North-East Wind)

The 'black north-easter' is the cruellist wind that Whitstable has to endure. With the flat shoreline, the close proximity of the Thames and Medway estuaries has made possible the unique spectacle of Whitstable's frozen coastline in severe winters. It is certain that this has happened from time immemorial. Indeed in the reign of Charles II in 1683 the Thames itself was frozen over from 4 December of that year for six weeks and on Christmas eve a fair was held on the frozen Thames; there can be no doubt that Whitstable suffered likewise all those 303 years ago.

But we are concerned with the photographic history of the town. It was in February 1895 that the first frozen sea was photographed and about eight photographs exist of that event.

The sea has frozen along the Whitstable shore seven times since then and a selection of the 95 frozen sea photographs in the collection are reproduced here, many for the first time.

We nearly landed in trouble when we photographed the 1940 frozen sea as the military authorities deemed they could be useful to the enemy, although they showed no defence works. Printing was immediately stopped but it made us very careful until the end of the war.

It is a most awesome sight to see the frozen sea for the first time. There is an eerie silence all along the coast. The cry of a lone gull only seems to intensify the silence and stillness. The spray of the waves freezes like soap flakes and on shore the ice can be three feet thick in places. Fishermen stand around and wonder how long it is going to last. In 1929 the crew of the oyster watch boat were unable to return ashore, it was impossible to row through the ice and a power boat was sent to tow them in to a welcoming crowd on the East Quay.

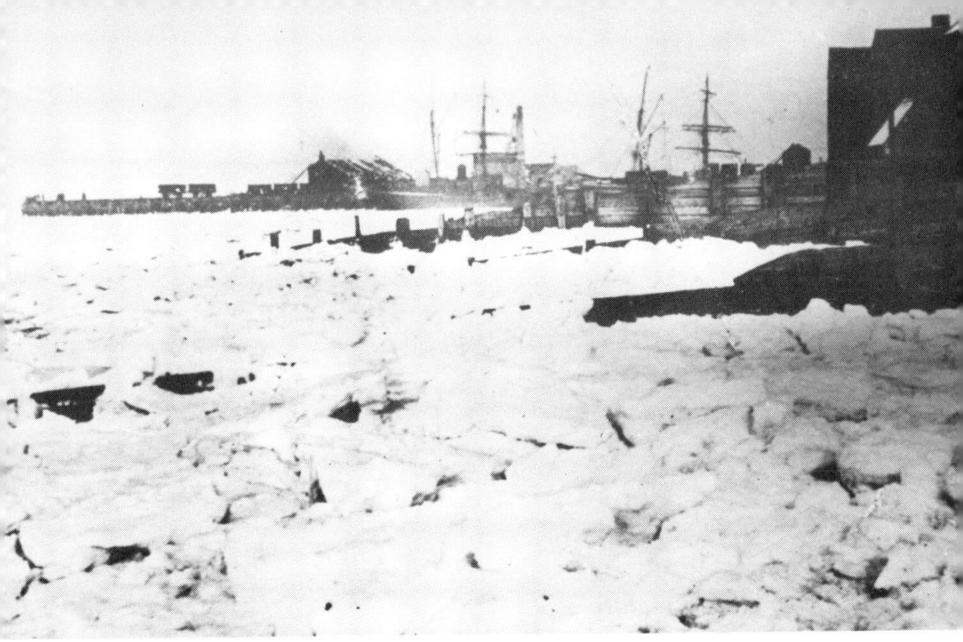

February 1895

Showing the entrance to the Harbour and Reeves Beach during the first photographically recorded frozen sea at Whitstable. The original chimney to the engine house and coal trucks can be seen on the East Quay.

A Thames barge and numerous oyster boats frozen in the ice. Nothing could move in these conditions.

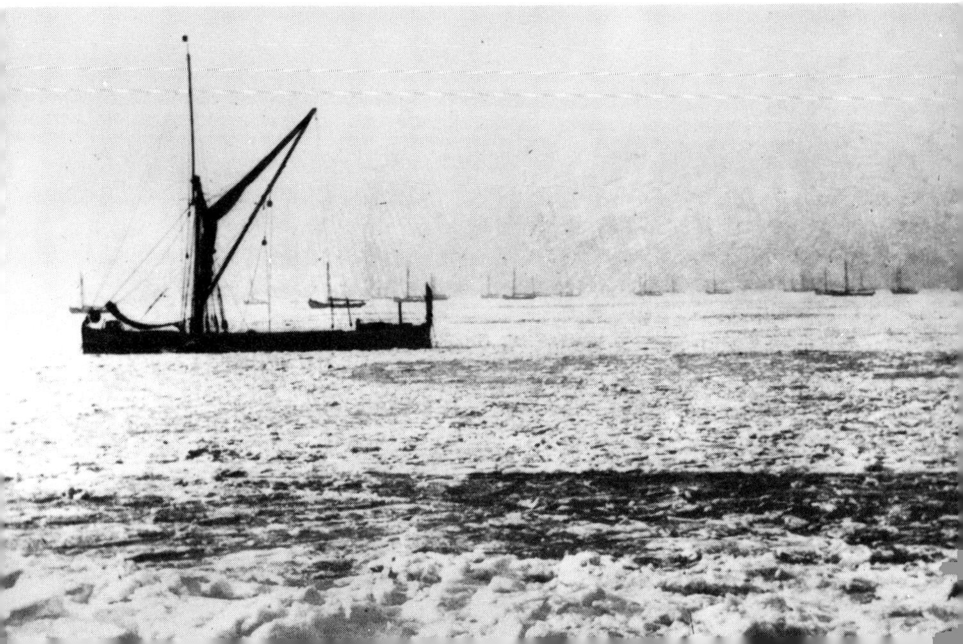

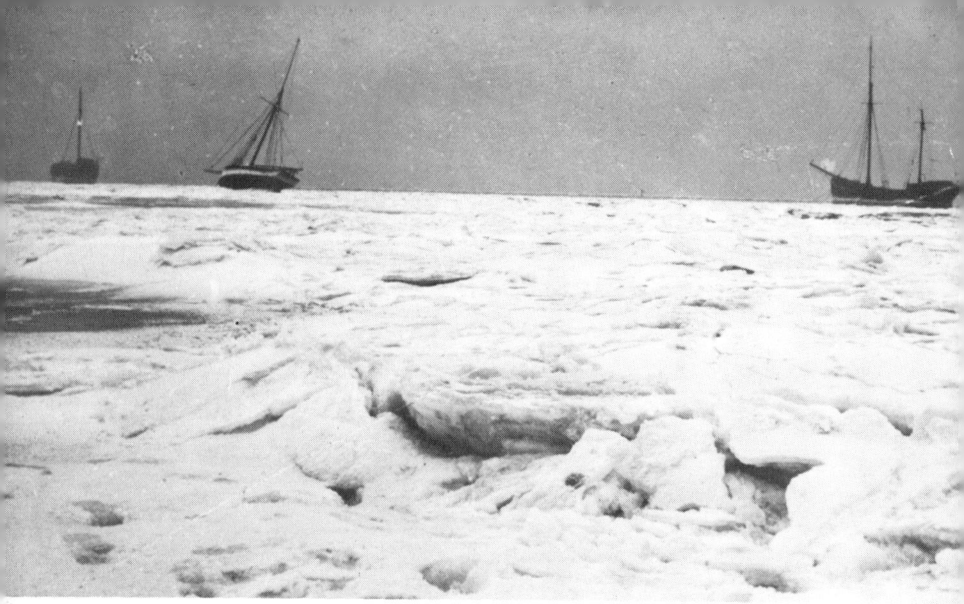

15 February 1929

As far as the eye can see a waste of ice and snow photographed in 1929.

An oyster boat and crew photographed against the flat shoreline of Seasalter.

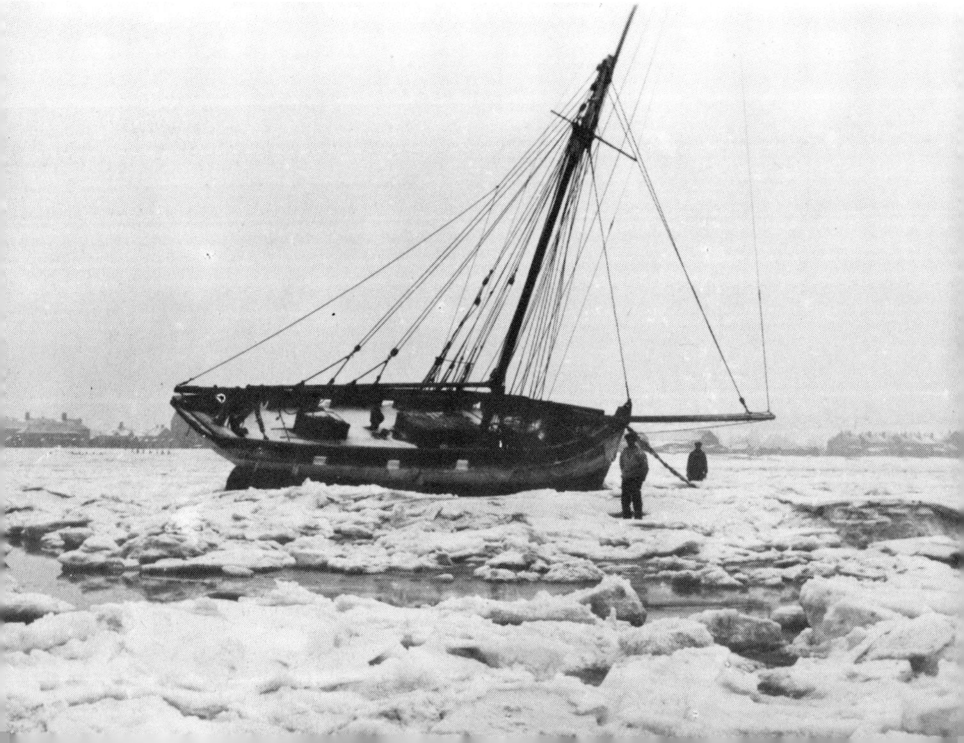

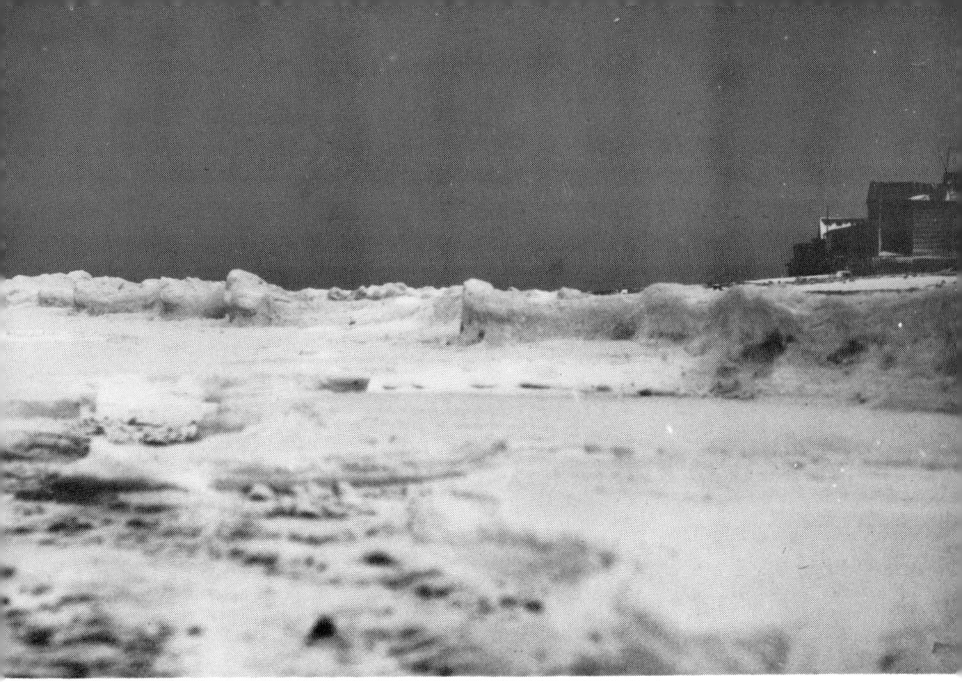

20 December 1938

In 1938 Christmas was ushered in by a severe frost that froze the sea – just a few months before World War II came to test our courage even more.

Three days later huge blocks of ice and snow line the shore.

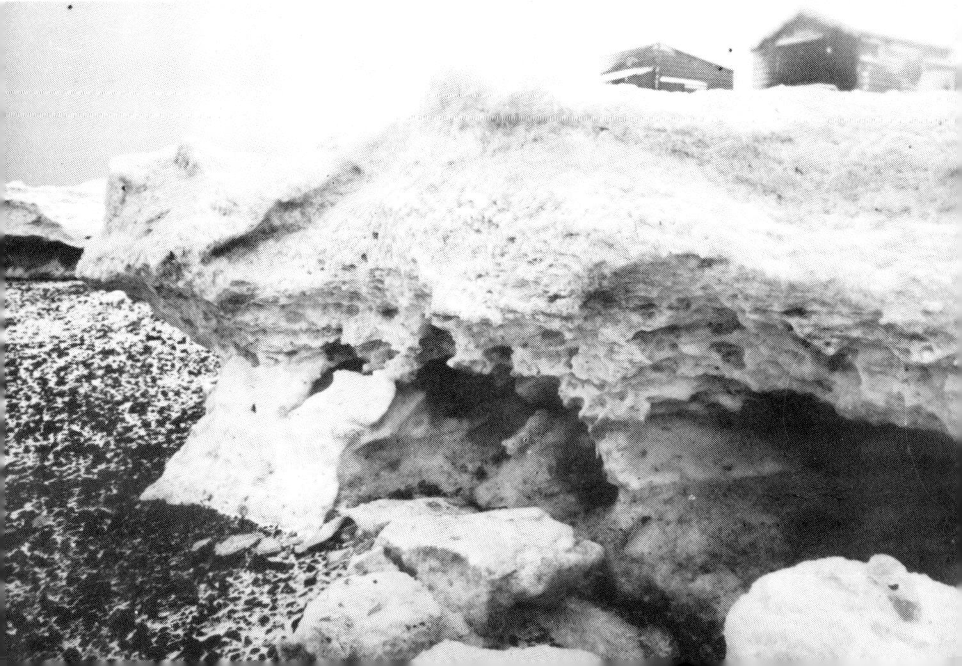

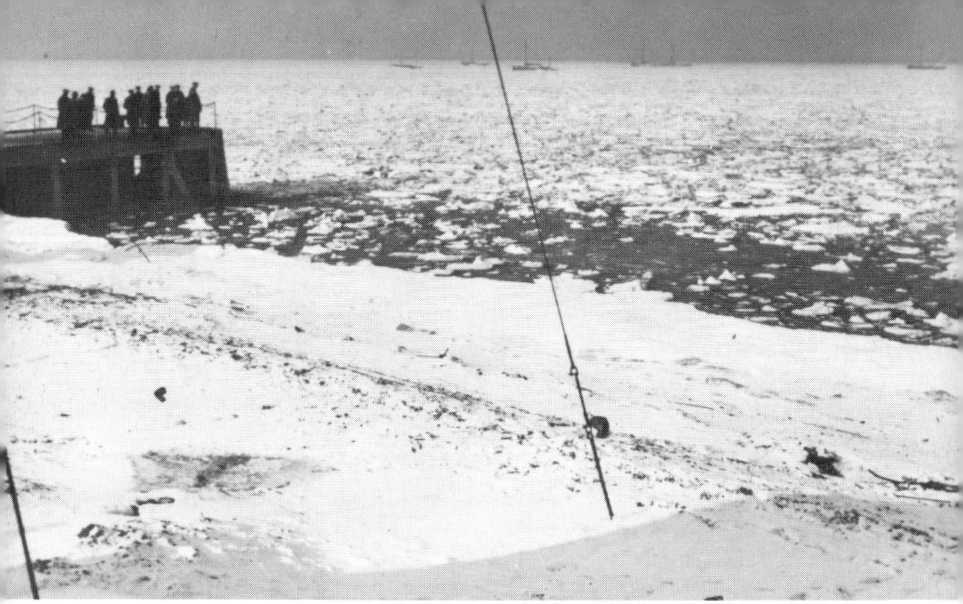

18 January 1940

World War II was a few months old when severe weather again hit Whitstable and this photograph shows the frozen fore-shore along the West Beach.

The following three photographs were taken five days later on the 23rd January and the ice shows no thaw.

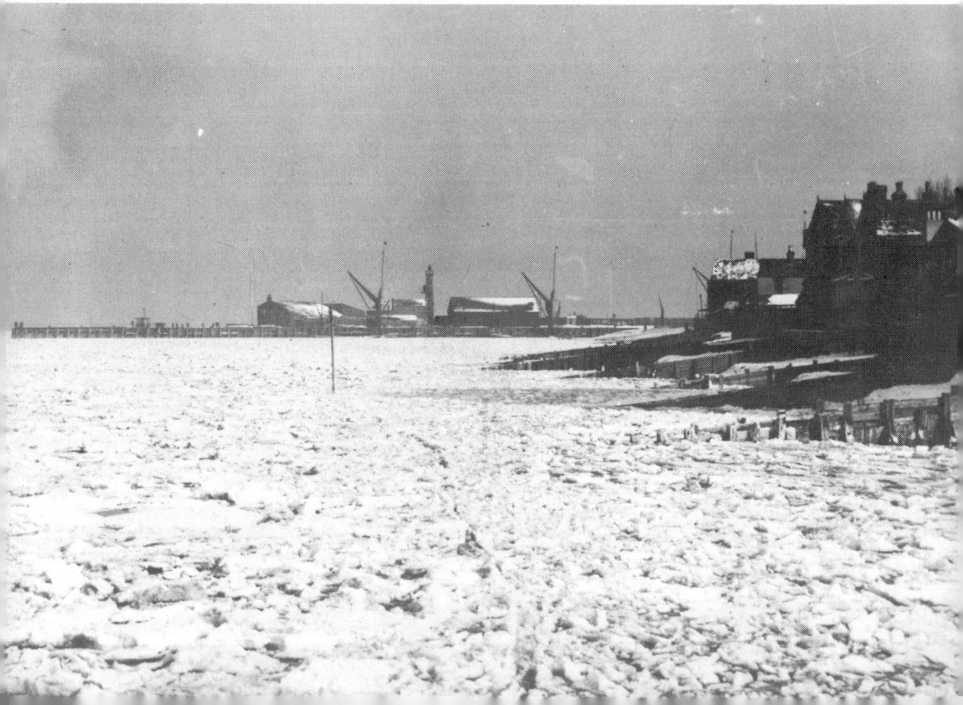

23 January 1940

Bathing cabins on Tankerton Beach look out over a hostile sea and a solitary gas lamp seemingly stays guard over a midnight dip!

Three feet thick blocks of ice and snow show the severity of the weather at this time. These are the photographs that had to be withdrawn from publication because of possible value to the enemy.

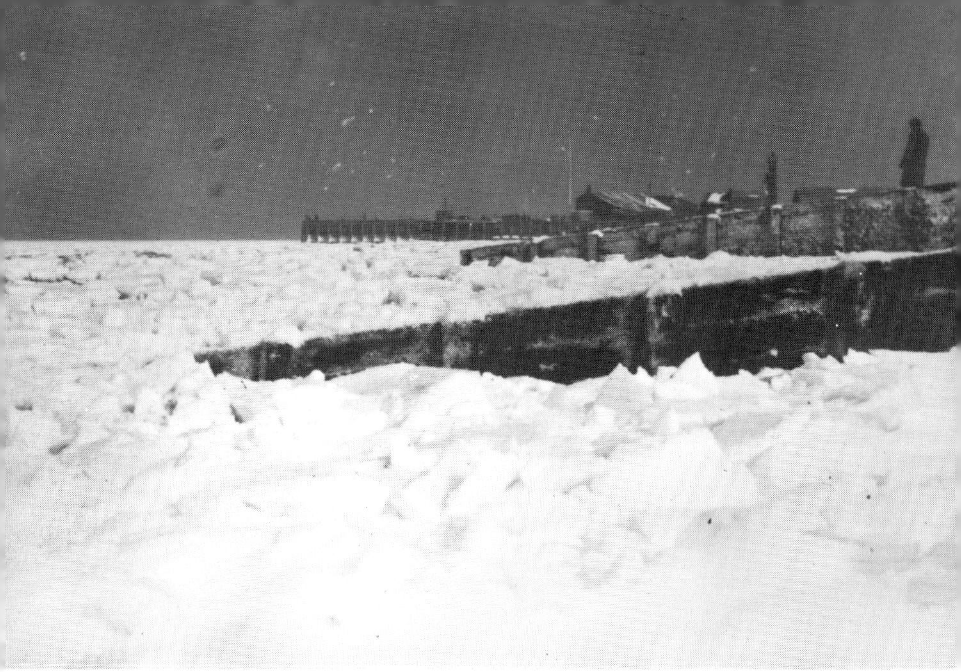

24 February 1947

A familiar sight now, soon after the end of the Second World War. This photograph shows the entrance to the harbour and Reeves Beach.

Wave Crest is the background to blocks of snow and ice on the West Beach.

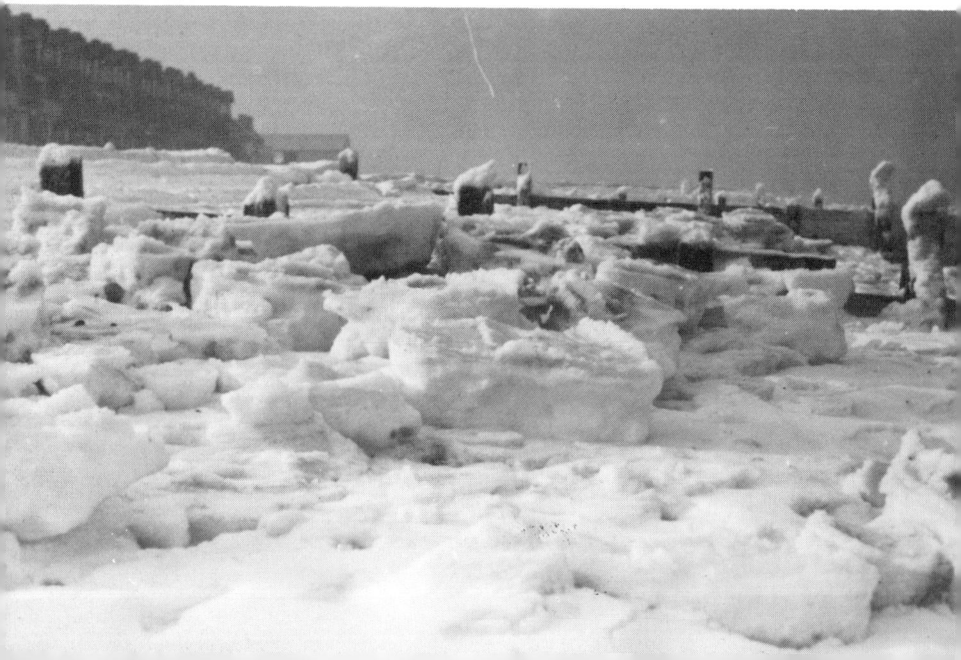

24 February 1947

The "Old Neptune" is the background here and stands defiant to all the elements.

Ice three feet thick in front of Marine Terrace on the West Beach. Pale green and transparent it was an awesome sight. The figure in the centre of the photograph is Mr. Derek Spratt, later to become the Editor of the "Whitstable Times".

4 February 1956

The frozen sea in the Harbour showing the corn silo on the West Quay which, a few months later, suffered a wall collapse on the 14 July 1956 when 120 tons of grain cascaded on to the quay. It has now been demolished.

The frozen waves at the Horsebridge. The Whitstable Oyster Co's premises in the background.

4 February 1956

A similar scene on the West Beach and a now demolished Boat Yard Slipway. A reminder of the byegone industry that was the backbone of Whitstable's prosperity.

The frozen waves with the "Old Neptune" and the Sea Cadets training ship "Vigilant" in the background.

Two years later. A view from the Horsebridge towards Seasalter taken at sunset.

26 January 1963

The East and West Quays of the Harbour frozen in with the cargo ship "Resurgence" moored alongside the East Quay.

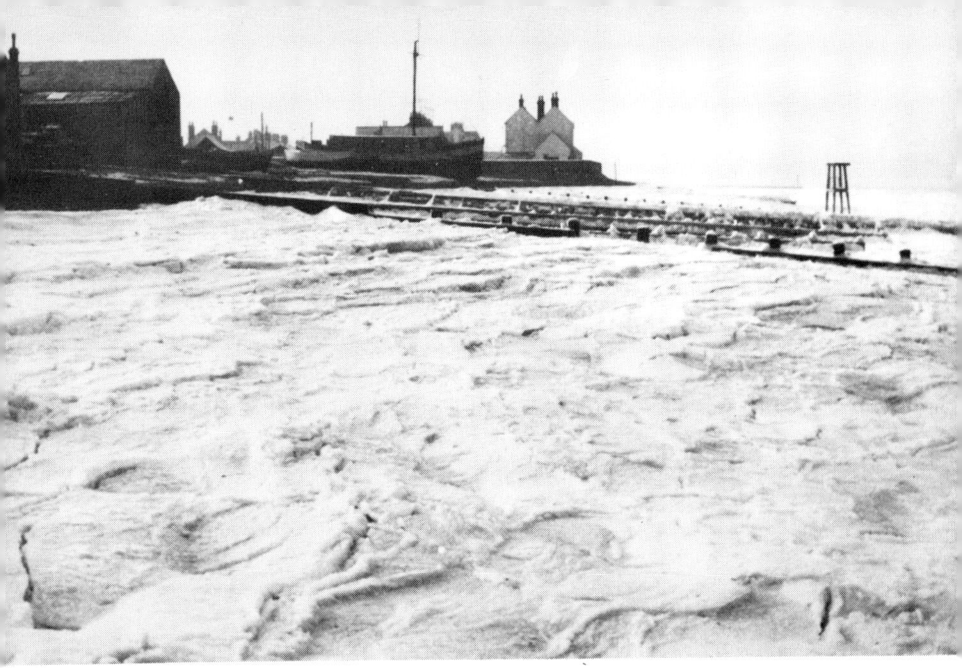

26 January 1963

Reeves Beach with a background of fishermens' huts, the training ship "Vigilant" and the "Old Neptune".

The uncanny silence of the frozen waves. The Whitstable Oyster Co's stores on the Horsebridge on the extreme right.

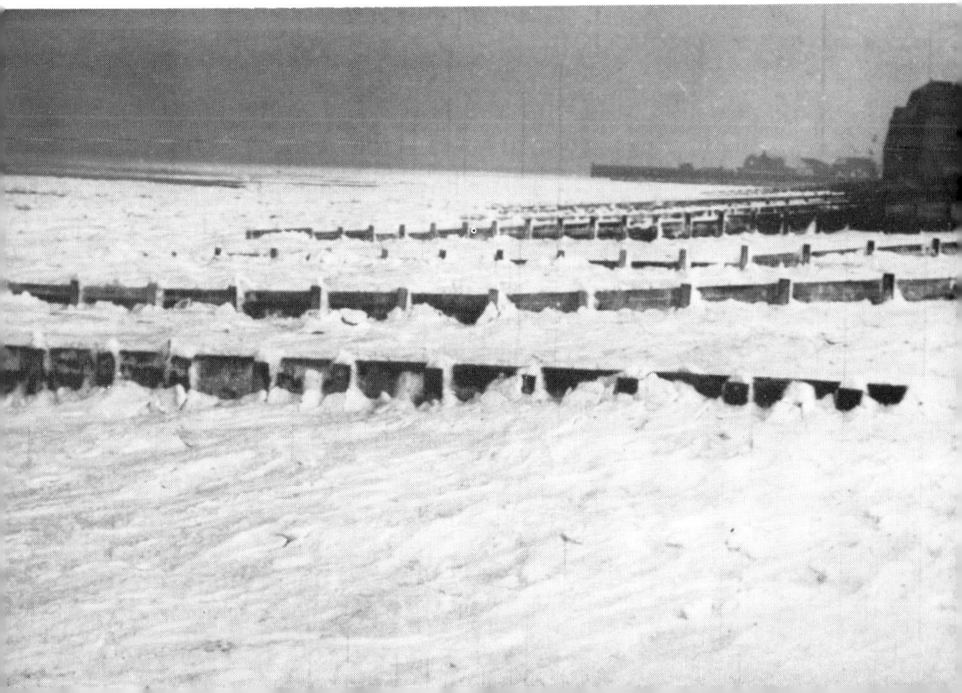

GALES

These few photographs are graphic evidence of the cruel winds which Whitstable has to endure from time to time. Gales like this must have inspired Charles Kingsley to write his "Ode to the North East Wind". Terrific seas must have accompanied the gales and some of these photographs were taken only six years after the great flood of 1897.

Apart from frozen seas and disastrous floods Whitstable from time to time had to withstand severe gales that have done much damage to property along the sea front. This photograph taken on 12 March 1903, shows the front of one of the numerous boat yards and stores torn out; a boat is seen blown up onto the beach.

A boat here, in full sail, is seen being blown up onto the beach by a severe gale.

One of the many tea huts on Tankerton Beach blown over in front of the Clock House which was at the end of the famous tea booths which were such a well-known feature of this part of Whitstable. It was burnt down in 1915.

The cruel north-easter here seen tearing at the fishermens' huts and stores. A Thames barge is up on the beach.

This photograph taken c1920 on the West Beach shows members of a little known club. Mr. Weston was a good swimmer — he is shown here with a polo ball — and water polo was often played here during the summer months. Mr. Weston had a shop 31 Harbour Street which was the old "Red Lion" public house which was burnt down in 1866. His daughter ran a hairdressers business at the same address, and he was sometime manager of the "Duke of Cumberland" hotel. The author was at one time a member of this club. A boxing ring was established in the basement and Billy Dadd and Ossie Foad trained here. It is remarkable that these premises have long been hairdressing salons. Mr. Teg Mullard was for many years a hairdresser here and still lives in the town.

This early aerial photograph which was taken in the 1920's shows the commencement of development of Swalecliffe. Right at the bottom of the left-hand corner are the old Black Cottages with their association with the Whitstable copperas industry. In the centre is Kite Farm — farmed at this time by the Pout family and just below on the right-hand side of the road is the old "Plough" public house. Out towards the sea Sea View Camp, a large caravan site, now occupies a large part of this area as the roadway — not much more than a track at this time, bends round to the old Coastguard Cottages on the right. On the right of the photograph the area is now covered by the new "Plough" public house, Russell Drive, Goodwin Avenue and the Colewood Industrial Estate.

Whitstable Swimming Club

Kite Farm, Swalecliffe

A cottage 'Shepherds Cot' here photographed in the 1930's has now been demolished. It was situated in what is now Castle Road almost opposite the bottom of Queens Road. When it was demolished more than two hundredweight of iron manacles were discovered under the floorboards. These were from the French prisoners who were all chained together during the war with Revolutionary France (1792-1802) in the reign of George III. After landing on the 'Street' at Tankerton they would make their way inland at night to 'Shepherds Cot' where their chains were removed. The two little girls in the photograph, in their Convent School uniforms, are Mary and Pamela Broadbridge who lived at the cottage in the 1930's.

This photograph shows the scene at the unveiling of the War Memorial draped with the Union Jack on the 1st April 1920. Many changes have been made since that time. The County Library and Lecture Room have replaced the old Council Offices which were originally built as a private house for Jonas King and named Oxford House in 1797. The iron railings too have gone and the whole area landscaped. The flagpole too has disappeared and the houses in the background have all been altered to shop fronts. The second house from the left is the home of Mr. Geo. Edward Foad who built the Salvation Army Hall, the Parish Hall in Oxford Street and the Catholic Church in Northwood Road. He also restored the Swalecliffe Church of St. John the Baptist in 1875. The War Memorial was designed by Mr. Frederick Browning of 50 Canterbury Road whose son Lieut. Browning is honoured among the dead on the Memorial. The Memorial takes the shape of a granite column on a square base containing 178 names of the dead of World War I and a scroll honouring the dead of World War II. On the top of the column is a lamp design topped with a cross. Mr. Browning's house in Canterbury Road is unique in that it has a milestone in the front garden.

Refuge for the French Prisoners of War

Unveiling the War Memorial in Oxford Street, 1920

Hop Pickers

A photograph taken probably around 1900 in Canterbury Road showing the typical annual hop picking exodus. Farm carts piled high with everything except the kitchen sink. The children all on their school summer holiday precariously perched on top of all the household necessities required for their life in the next week or so in the hop fields. The most likely venue would be in the Faversham, Dargate and Boughton area. The money earned on these occasions was a much welcome addition to the weekly income as at this time there was much poverty in the town. All this activity has of course now ceased as the hops are now stripped by mechanical power.

The lower photograph shows a group of Swalecliffe hop pickers photographed in 1903 and includes the Richard, Champs, Keen, Tritton and Gisby families. The photograph was taken at Frogs Island Farm which is between Chestfield and Herne. Owing to the proximity of this farm to Chestfield it is more than probable the hops were processed at the oast house at Chestfield, as it is known that hops were processed there in the early part of the century. The oast house is now converted into two separate dwelling houses, close to the 14th century barn which was part of the old Balsar Street Farm.

Mr. Robert H. Goodsall and Mr. Wallace Harvey
in Reeves Alley, High Street

Mr. Robert H. Goodsall is here seen examining the flint wall at No. 76 High Street. This is part of the very thick wall of the stables of the Customs Riding Officer who occupied the building during the vast smuggling activities that were rife in the eighteenth and nineteenth centuries on this part of the Kent coast. Reeves Alley is between the Salvation Army Hall and No. 76 High Street. Messrs. Bartlett and Bisson's Dairies had a shop here before World War II and when they vacated the premises the foundations were thoroughly examined and excavated.

Dr.C.E.Etheridge, M.B.E., M.B.Lond., M.R.C.S., L.R.C.P. London

Many Whitstable people will have been grateful for the lifetime devotion to their welfare by Dr. Etheridge. He was truly of the sea being a founder member of the Whitstable Yacht Club in 1904 and Commodore in 1911 and continued in that capacity for more than 30 years. Born in 1874 in Hertfordshire the family came to Whitstable about a year later where his father, Dr. Charles Etheridge, took up a practice in the town. They lived in 'Ivy House' Oxford Street a large 17/18th century building that had smuggling associations, having secret tunnels and cupboards. The house was demolished in the early years of this century. It occupied a site that is now the infants school behind the bus stop in Oxford Street. Dr. Etheridge was a childhood friend of Somerset Maugham and is mentioned as the local doctor in his book "Cakes and Ale". He was awarded the M.B.E. in 1951 for his services to the town. There was a family connection with Nelson and his grandfather Edward Etheridge collected many relics of the great admiral, but most were collected by Dr. Etheridge from all over the country. The family originated in Norfolk and he died at his home 'Norfolk Cottage' Tankerton Road in 1962.

The Old Forge, Swalecliffe

Post Office and "Fan" Public House

This is the only known photograph of the Swalecliffe forge in the early 1900's before the development of the Swalecliffe shopping area. It was a weatherboard building with slate roof and the usual forge chimney. It was built in the front of two brick built cottages which today are the Forge Tea Rooms. The roadway has now been extensively widened and the wide grass verge has disappeared. About this time the forge and Forge House were occupied by William Silk and Albert Sinclair. In more modern times Cllr. Geo Vickery occupied the premises.

STEPHEN DOUGLAS WEST (1880-1945)

Mr. Stephen West, who made many of these inset photographs, had his photographers shop and studio at No. 47 Oxford Street. He had moved from St. Peter's in Thanet in May 1914. Many of these inset photographs were made during the first two years of World War I. They were Victorian in their concept and are now collectors pieces. It was a simple double printing technique incorporating an inset photograph, often a loved one on the Western Front in France. This was copied and printed with the portrait taken in the studio. There must be many of these photographs in the town, the photograph here reproduced is an unknown portrait.

A close up view of the old Swalecliffe Post Office which seems to consist of nothing more than a corrugated iron-roofed lean-to. The only indication that it is indeed a post office is an enamelled plate on the cottage whose garden is adorned with a wealth of lilies. The old "Fan" public house is the weatherboard building right on the bend in the roadway.

Rather a posed picture but it graphically shows the Whitstable oyster fishermen in the early years of the century, wearing the thick woollen jerseys, the leather knee boots (no rubber in those days) and the traditional peaked cap, bringing oysters ashore to load into the two-wheeled tip-up cart for hauling up the beach and on to the sorting and packing shed.

WALTER CAMBURN

This old tramp was often to be seen in Whitstable in the 1920's begging for scraps and clothing. Known as Walter Skimps he lived in a tin shed in Clowes Wood, his only companion was a cat which he tethered on a piece of string. He was a kindly old man and harmed no one. Of a religious nature it was thought that he was a seafarer as he always wore a cheesecutter hat. He was unwashed and was always to be seen with his long stout stick.

The Leggatt brothers' fishing boat F70 moored in the harbour entrance with a World War II mine, which snagged in their nets, lashed to the bows. Invariably these contact mines were towed out to deep water where they were exploded by a bomb disposal team. The Leggatt brothers were the first to use echo sounding equipment to locate the huge shoals of sprats which were fished in these waters for a number of years after World War II.

Oyster Fishermen

The Leggatt Brothers

BOMB DAMAGE
1939 – 1945

*"Wherefore men fight not as they fought
In the brave days old"*

Lord Macaulay
"Horatius" (Days of Ancient Rome)

Traumatic years which left their mark on Whitstable. Much property was demolished in the Victoria Street—Regent Street area when a large mine was dropped during the evening of 11 October 1941. Scars have healed somewhat since that date and it is now the site of the Victoria Street car park. But before this, early one morning, German bombers flew so low over Tankerton that the black crosses on the fuselage were plainly visible and as they were watched from an upstairs window they imparted no fear — it was the first raid on the town. As the bombers rose over the town suddenly bomb doors opened and a stick of bombs were released which fell in the Regent Street—Warwick Road area demolishing a few houses.

The following photographs were specially taken to the order of the authorities with the stipulation that they were not for publication. Two prints from each negative had to accompany the negatives which were handed to the Whitstable Urban District Council. Fifty five photographs were taken during the course of the war and when hostilities ended all negatives were handed back. This is the first time they have been published and the photographic history of Whitstable during the last hundred years would not be complete were they omitted.

It is a grim reminder of what the Whitstable people had to endure during those terrible years. They were taken by my father and myself before joining the Royal Air Force in 1941. As far as I am aware no Whitstable photographs exist of the Battle of Britain, when the blue September skies in 1940 were covered in the vapour trails of the Spitfires and Hurricanes as they circled the hordes of German bombers. But many Whitstable people will remember those days when the roofs of Whitstable were showered with the cartridge cases of spent ammunition and the sight of the pilots' victory rolls to be called a little later by Churchill's immortal words "The Few". We will be everlastingly grateful to them.

The corner of Terrys Lane (named after Thomas Terry in 1846) and Horsebridge Road. The East Kent Road Car Co's booking office and houses in Terrys Lane are destroyed. The booking office was moved next door in the old garage which was Woods Motor Garage in the 1920's.

The whole side of this bungalow in Swalecliffe Road was torn out and the bomb crater filled with water.

This is the rear of houses in Regent Street destroyed on 13 August 1940.

Only the fireplace and chimney stack remain upright of this large house in Ham Shades Lane.

A huge mine which fell on a fish shop at the junction of Regent Street and Victoria Street on 11 October 1941 made a large crater and demolished many buildings. The area is now Victoria Street car park.

Another view showing Victoria Street and Bexley Street in the background. Victoria Street flats have now been built on the site of the houses on the right.

A huge hole is torn in the Assembly Rooms on Horsebridge Road and a small cafe is demolished. On the extreme right is the fire station which was located here during the war.

This is the rear of No. 5 High Street (a wine merchant) which is next to the Bear & Key Hotel, and was the only bomb to fall in the High Street.

This bomb which fell in Newton Road, Tankerton, pierced reinforced concrete and has blown a blister in the roadway. Note that there are no broken windows in the house nearby.

No. 3 and No. 5 Warwick Road are demolished leaving the gas lamp unscathed.

A row of bungalows in Diamond Road is destroyed. They have all been rebuilt.

Houses are destroyed here in Acton Road an area of high density.

This is at Bartletts Corner in Church Street. The whole of the side and front of this house is ripped away. The entrance to Bridewell Park now occupies this site in Ham Shades Lane.

The huge crater formed by a mine dropped behind Joy Lane. Another mine was dropped on the shore in front of Wave Crest but little damage was done. Children play in the crater.

Mrs. Emma Godfrey came to Whitstable just after the first World War with her two sons, William and Wallace, from Devon where the family had a florists business in Ottery St. Mary. Wallace was trained in Kew Gardens and a shop was opened at No. 17 Harbour Street. William is seen here outside the Harbour Street shop with giant marrows grown by Mr. Davidson of the Manor House. They weighed almost half a hundredweight each. The Godfreys later had a shop at No. 7 Oxford Street, now the Farm Shop, and a nursery in Harwich Street trading as E. Godfrey and Sons. They were one of the first florists in the town.

This cinema and concert hall on the corner of Harbour Street and Victoria Street was, during the 1914-18 war, one of the three cinemas showing the early silent films such as 'The Exploits of Elaine' and 'The Clutching Hand' etc. which were in serial form. The heroine was always left in fear of her life and it was imperative to go the following week to see how she got out of it! Later, in the 1920's, it was the venue for concert parties, particularly the 'Leadswingers'. The owner was Mr. Edwin Chinnick. One of his attractions was the appearance of 'Lady Little' the doll lady, a tiny girl age 22 who stood only about 3 feet tall. The photograph shows the stage of the Palais de Luxe bedecked as a harvest festival display. No photographs can be found of the exterior of the theatre. The 'Palais' was opened on December 8th 1913. Purchased by Mr. Chinnick in 1925 it finally closed in 1931. Mr. Hector Davey purchased the premises the following year and opened them as furniture salesrooms. During the 1914-18 War the 'Palais' was used as a recruiting office for the armed forces. Today the premises have been converted to a shopping arcade.

Mr. William Godfrey, Florist

Palais de Luxe Cinema

Mr. Hubbard outside his shop at 37 Harbour Street complete with the usual down-to-the-ground white apron. This shop was later to be part of the Palais de Luxe cinema and concert hall, managed by Mr. Chinnick. To the right of Mr. Lawson was Ridouts the printers and stationers who were at No. 36 for many years. The printing works — the buildings are still there — are at the back of the premises. In 1932 after the Palais de Luxe closed Mr. H. Davey had the premises as a furniture showroom. Lately it has become an arcade of shops. Opposite these premises was the "Red Lion" public house which was burnt down in 1867, two years before the great fire of Harbour Street.

This photograph taken at the turn of the century shows that Harbour Street was composed almost wholly of shops. On the extreme right was Ridouts stationers and printing works and next to them two shops were to become the Palais de Luxe cinema and concert hall. On the corner of Victoria Street was the Harbour Street post office later to become Blaxlands greengrocers. Harbour Street at this time was a very busy area, catering for the shipping and fishing industry of the Harbour. Further down the street opposite the "Nelson" Inn was the "Royal Native" public house and the "Spread Eagle". The church of the Harbour Street Christian Fellowship now stands there. This very long street, which stretches from the "Bear & Key" hotel to the commencement of Northwood Road is characterised by the very narrow section which necessitates it being a one-way street in these days of the motor car.

Harbour Street Supply Stores

Harbour Street

The narrowness of Herne Bay Road is shown in this photograph taken in the early 1920's of the bridge over Swalecliffe Brook which has not far to go to enter the sea. The tall building in the centre of the photograph and the cottage in front is the old post office and "Fan" public house. The motor car is an early Morris Oxford owned by Stephen West the author's father.

An aerial photograph taken about 1925 showing the development of Chestfield by Mr. Geo Reeves. In the centre are the tennis courts now occupied by Dormy House No. 105 and Upper Meadow No. 107 Chestfield Road. The road on the extreme left is Molehill Road with the three houses Revel House, Molehill Cottage and Sparrer Court.

The first and eighteenth hole of the Chestfield Golf Club on the extreme right is marked by a couple of bunkers. The holes were originally reversed to the present day layout, the first hole being on the left and the eighteenth on the right of the photograph. In the top right hand corner just to the left of the Oast House is 'Long Wall' built by Mr. Geo Reeves and occupied by his daughter Greta who married Mr. Lamb of "Uncle Dick" Daily Mirror fame. The "Bell House" and "Brown Butts" had by this time been built and a little later the tiny Chestfield Telephone Exchange was built almost on the corner of Molehill Road, followed in recent years by a large modern automatic exchange.

In the foreground of the lower photograph taken in the mid 1920's is the site of the original Chestfield Bowling Green. The ground is now occupied by part of 107 and 109 Chestfield Road, which is opposite the Bell House. Mr. George Reeves and Mr. Stanley Reeves can be seen playing here. Molehill Cottage is in the background.

Beach Road

Dan Sherrin

This photograph was taken just before the bazaars and lock-up shops in Beach Road were demolished. Mr. Dadd had a bazaar on the opposite side of the road as well as the shoe shop depicted here. Jacques Arcade was on the left a little further along. The site today is occupied by modern commercial buildings. In the summer these amusement arcades and parks were thronged with holidaymakers — the area was only a couple of minutes walk from the Whitstable—Canterbury railway station.

Another look at the irrepressible Daniel Sherrin who lived at "Westbank" Joy Lane. An accomplished landscape artist in oils he often carved models, fireplaces, etc. He even made his own coffin which he ceremoniously lowered into a trench excavated for main laying in Joy Lane. Here he is seen with an aeroplane he constructed which almost certainly never flew. A continual smoker, a heavy drinker and an eccentric dresser — he once wore the Oxford Bags famous in the 1930's with their 36 inch trouser bottoms. His wager to stop the London train at the bottom of his garden was a story that was well known. He was fined £5 (the penalty for improper use) and still made a profit. He had one son, also an artist, but in water colours, who lived in Herne Bay. It is not known who the man on the left is.

Dollar Row

Oxford Street

Dollar Row, so named because, legend has it, that the six cottages were built with the proceeds of the sale of dollars raised from a sunken galleon which foundered off the Irish coast in 1588. The story is discredited by Mr. Porter a descendent of Mr. John Gann who built the cottages. Altogether 25,000 dollars were recovered from the old wreck. Whitstable divers were engaged on this wreck and there is no doubt that in those days diving was most profitable. The wooden casks had rotted away leaving the dollars still in a barrel shape. The old "Kings Head" public house is at the end of this row of cottages, for many years now a private residence. In January 1852 the landlord of the "Kings Head" together with the landlord of the "Hoy" were fined 10/- and £1 respectively for being open after hours on December 27th 1851. This photograph shows Dollar Row on the right with the old "Kings Head" a little farther along.

Photographed c1880, this photograph of Oxford Street taken from the tower of St. Alphege Church shows on the left the Wesleyan school-room which was built in 1874 (St. John's Methodist Church was built six years earlier and opened by the Rev. F. J. Johnson D.D. on 22 October 1868). Immediately to the right of this can be seen the Foresters Hall, originally in 1862, a school-room. It was added to in 1882 and became the meeting place of the Ancient Order of Foresters and recently purchased for the town as a museum. For many years it was the H.Q. of the Royal British Legion which has now moved to 61 Oxford Street (opposite the "East Kent" public house).

Immediately beneath the Wesleyan school-room can be seen a long low black building with a single stack chimney at the end and at the rear of Cheadles. This building was originally Haywards rope works which stretched right across what is now Regent Street. In more recent times mineral water was manufactured here — the proprietor at one time was Mr. W. London.

On the opposite side of the road can be seen the junction of Middle Wall and Oxford Street. The tiny cottage there is now replaced by Chester House (next to Days Garage). Sheep can be seen grazing on the 'Salts' now the Seasalter Golf Club which was established in 1909.

The office and shop of Amos and Foad, 45 Oxford Street, c1907, builders in the town from the 1860's having built major public buildings from that time. The notice in the window is offering land for sale in Kent Street at 35/- per foot with roads, paths and drains paid for. Later on the shop was owned by Mr. Amers in 1914 confectioners and news-agents and later still by Andrews and Luckhursts. Today it is a Chiropractic Clinic.

Schoolgirls of the 1890's photographed outside the school-room doorway, a number of them wearing the workmanlike pinafore. Girls as well as boys were educated here at this time. It was a time of real hardship in the town and any severe weather made attendance very difficult or impossible. This photograph was taken before 1893 as the boys afterwards occupied the whole school with Mr. George Kirkby as the Headmaster, a post he held for 40 years. The teacher on the left of the photograph is Miss L. Carlton, the same teacher as depicted on pages 36 and 37 in the first book "Portrait of a Seaside Town". Miss Carlton married Mr. George Spendiff, a tobacconist of 71 High Street, Whitstable. She is the mother of the author's wife. The teacher on the right is unknown — it would be interesting to discover who she is, it may be poss-ible to identify some of the children also.

Mr. George Edward Foad

Board School, Oxford Street

The Town Bus was a railway public service vehicle which was in use in Whitstable. This derelict vehicle was photographed by the author in the grounds of Court Lees, Pean Hill. It was a four wheeled horse drawn bus and almost certainly in use at the turn of the century. The advent of the motor car ended its use in the town. Also at this time horse-drawn landaus were available for hire; they would be stationed on the cab rank along Canterbury Road near the bridge which was, of course, the railway station before 1913. The one illustrated is a cane seated vehicle photographed in Canterbury Road and one would have to use umbrellas if it rained! This method of travelling too has given way to the motor taxi. Landaus at this time were the popular means of travel at weddings, etc., the driver's whip always adorned with a white ribbon bow.

The Town Bus

Landau in Canterbury Road

Church Street Village Cricket Club

Whitstable Goal Running Club

Taken in 1933, this photograph shows the Church Street Cricket Club which has now been disbanded and the playing field situated opposite the old parsonage has been built over, mainly by Summerfield Avenue. Mr. J. Crawfurd Platt was the President who lived in 'Summerfield' and owned the playing field and the headquarters were at the "Monument" Inn. There were many well known Whitstable members amongst whom the following will be recognised. Front row: M. Broadbridge, G. Munday, W. G. T. Pearse, J. Rhodes. Second row: Mrs. Harris, D. Simpson, S. Harris, H. Pope (capt.), J. Winkel, Mabel Poole. Third row: Mr. Ferguson, A. R. Harris, C. O. T. Witty, T. Castle, Mr. Hepburn, P. J. Trinder (sec.), Mr. Rhodes. Back row: N. Platt (chairman), W. Rigden, P. Harris, L. Davey, R. Harris.

A later photograph of this club, a sport unique in the district. Clubs were also formed in Herne Bay and Faversham and competitions were held between them. Many older members of Whitstable will be able to recognise some of the men in this photograph taken c1910. Mr. W. Dadd who had a shoe shop in Harbour Street is seen sitting on the ground in a dark shirt.

This photographic record would not be complete if the concert parties that were popular in the early years of the 20th century were not included. 'The Leadswingers' concert party performed at the Palais de Luxe in Harbour Street. Mr. Chinnick was the proprietor of the 'Palais' at this time.

Sited on the Tankerton Slopes, opposite the Tankerton Hotel, the Lawn Pavilion too was popular, the 'Jollity Boys' in particular. Sandy Sandford concert party also put on concerts here and a photograph from his production of 'Aladdin' is reproduced here. The Lawn Pavilion at this time in the 1920's was a substantial building — a far cry from the original tiny hut. All is now gone of course and the area is now a picnic site owned by the City Council.

Concert Parties

Street Party

The Flying Dutchman Championships held in Whitstable in 1959.

V. E. Day street parties were very popular in celebrating the end of World War II. This one in Suffolk Street was typical, grown ups as well as children enjoying themselves after years of privation. Amongst those recognised are the families of Mr. T. G. Mummery, Steve Carpenter, Hubbard, Mr. & Mrs. March, Pat Price (mother of Reg Price who now runs the "Jolly Sailor" public house at Seasalter). Mr. Hector Davey J.P. can be recognised with the trilby hat on the right. (Mr. Davey had a High Street drapers shop where Whites of Kent now are).

This photograph won for the author a Bronze Olympic Medallion in a Rome Exhibition of Olympic Sports during the 1960 Rome Olympics. One of only 12 from Great Britain, it shows the start of the 'Flying Dutchman' Class Yacht Race during the Flying Dutchman Championships held under the auspices of the Whitstable Yacht Club in 1959. It was, too, the only photograph illustrated from England in the official catalogue. The Championships were held in beautiful weather and were a tribute to the Whitstable Yacht Club members. Entries were received from all over the world including the Soviet Union. England won the National Championship and Capio of Italy won the World Championship. An interesting point is that the yacht in the foreground is crewed by two Dutchmen. The author specialised in photographing yachts and during this period produced many hundreds of yachting photographs, one being used as a Southern Railway poster advertising Whitstable.

INDEX

NOTES

NOTES

NOTES

NOTES

NOTES